/00

Bring Me the Ocean

Bring Me the Ocean

Nature as Teacher, Messenger,
and Intermediary

REBECCA A. REYNOLDS

VANDERWYK & BURNHAM
ACTON, MASSACHUSETTS

This publication is sold with the understanding that the publisher is not engaged in rendering legal, psychiatric, or other professional services. If expert assistance is required, the services of a competent professional person should be sought.

Published by VanderWyk & Burnham
A Division of Publicom, Inc.
Acton, Massachusetts

Publisher's Cataloging-in-Publication Data
Reynolds, Rebecca A.
Bring Me the Ocean: Nature as Teacher, Messenger,
and Intermediary / Rebecca A. Reynolds
1. Nature—Psychological aspects I. Title
2. Volunteer workers in mental health
BF 353.5.N37   155.9   94–61765
ISBN: 0-9641089-2-5

Acknowledgment is gratefully given for permission to include these works of others: **"The Peace of Wild Things"** from *Openings*, copyright © 1968 by Wendell Berry, reprinted by permission of Harcourt Brace & Company. **Line drawings** by Sarah Seabury Ward: v, vi, vii. **Nature photography** by Ivan Massar: 2-3, 4, 12, 18, 26-27, 28, 33, 36, 41, 54, 60, 62-63, 64, 67, 70, 75, 78, 82, 90-91, 92, 96. **Photo essay section:** Jane Caulfield—45 *lower right;* Todd Crocker—42, 49; Nancy Fuller—44 *bottom;* Lisa Luciano/Youville Hospital and Rehabilitation Center—45 *top;* Ivan Massar—43 *top,* 43 *middle left,* 43 *lower right,* 44 *top,* 48 *upper right;* Nancy Mattila—47 *bottom,* 48 *upper left;* Robert J. Remeika—47 *upper left;* Julia Summers—45 *lower left,* 46 *series,* 47 *middle right,* 48 *bottom.* **Afterword photography** by Julia Summers: 98.

Manufactured in the United States of America
10 9 8 7 6 5 4 3 2 1

Book design: Ruth Lacey Design

To my mother and father
for showing me the wild places.
To my brother
for the snapping turtles and eels.

Those who contemplate the beauty of the earth find reserves of strength that will endure as long as life lasts. There is symbolic as well as actual beauty in the migration of the birds, the ebb and flow of the tides, the folded bud ready for the spring. There is something infinitely healing in the repeated refrains of nature—the assurance that dawn comes after night, and spring after the winter.

—Rachel Carson, *The Sense of Wonder*

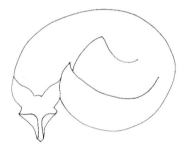

CONTENTS

ACKNOWLEDGMENTS

The tortoise was cold when I picked her up. Too cold. We were in the middle of loading the car for an early morning program at a hospital school. It was January in New England, and the tortoise needed to be warmed up as quickly as possible.

I tucked her in underneath my thick wool sweater. As long as I didn't move my arm too far from my body, she was snug in the warmth of my armpit and I could keep loading the car. But soon the hard-shelled creature gave a great wiggle and let loose, drenching my side with tortoise pee! By now it was snowing, my shirt was soaked, and we were late.

At times like this I wonder: How did I get into this? Then I smile, because I know full well how it began. It was my mother, Sarah.

As experiences like this led to the writing of the book, many people were involved in its evolution. I would especially like to thank Nancy Mattila and Bruce Detrick for their vision and belief in so many aspects of my life. Special thanks to those involved in Animals As Intermediaries—my co-workers, the corporation and board, volunteers, and especially Suzanne Ballard and Judith Scotnicki. I am deeply grateful to Barbara Whitesides and Giselle Weiss for their clarity, skill, and care in editing the book. Julia Summers, Ivan Massar, and Todd Crocker have documented the work of AAI with images over the years, for which I am indebted. Thank you to Meredith Rutter, Pat Moore, and Ruth Lacey for their commitment in bringing this book to completion. Most of all, to my friends and family who made it all possible, especially Sarah Seabury (Reynolds) Ward, thank you for your inspiration and support.

Introduction: A Sense of Place

AT A CHRONIC CARE HOSPITAL WE MET IRENE, an elderly Greek woman. Able to speak only her native Greek, she had become isolated by her inability to communicate with other residents. Over recent years she had gradually lapsed into silence. She had withdrawn so deeply that her silence extended even to her family. When they made their regular visits she rarely spoke with them, responding to their questions with a bare yes or no.

On this day we came with an ocean program. Along with sand and shells, we brought indoors thick piles of seaweed. When Irene saw the seaweed being lifted up out of the buckets, she wheeled her chair over, her expression shifting profoundly.

Picking up handfuls of the kelp, Irene smelled its saltiness and began weeping. Slowly, haltingly, she began to speak. None of us understood her Greek, but we all understood her joy. Such beauty lit her face as she poured forth descriptions of the ocean and her childhood home! We listened to the texture of her stories. We could clearly understand the context of what she said in the passion of her description.

Later that day when her family visited, Irene broke into lively discussion with them. Her family was amazed. *This* was Irene as they remembered her. They eagerly translated to the staff pieces of her conversation—her joy in smelling the salt of the wind off the ocean, held now in the brine of the seaweed. Her vivid memories of growing up on a small island in Greece, walking down its beaches. Of the fishing boats coming in at the end of the day, lit by sunset. Of nets hung out along the beach to dry and be mended. Of the meals each night gathering family and friends together.

We listened, and her joy infused us all.

This book grew out of stories like Irene's, in which the natural world is a bridge for connection among people, animals, and the environment. The stories that follow document the traveling program Animals As Intermediaries (AAI),* which visits hospitals and other closed-care institutions and brings animals, nature, and the arts to people who do not have ready access to the outdoors. The name implies an emphasis on animals; it is a name that has stayed with us from our beginnings. We work with companion animals, farm animals, and permanently injured wildlife. The wildlife come to us through veterinarians or licensed rehabilitators. Because of injuries or birth-related conditions, the wildlife are unable to survive in the wild. We are state and federally licensed to care for them. The animals we work with are, in a sense, intermediaries for experience and understanding—but equally so are the shells and kelp, the logs and rocks, the clay and stories.

AAI goes wherever people are isolated from direct contact with the natural world. The program works with the elderly in chronic care facilities, in nursing and psychiatric settings; with children born HIV-positive in inner-city hospitals; with children in hospital schools, and in day and residential treatment centers; with physically and/or emotionally challenged children and adults; with battered women and their children; with prisoners; with hospice patients.

In designing a day's program, we start with the season. Next we choose an environment and then work from there, adding secondary themes, such as the transition from day to night. We draw on the natural materials we find during outdoor "gatherings." We draw on the animals that are available to us that day, and on the requests we have received during prior programs. We may bring indoors a meadow in fall, a salt marsh during winter, or perhaps a forest's edge in spring.

---

*Animals As Intermediaries is a program of Seabury School, Inc., a nonprofit Massachusetts organization. Since 1983, AAI has provided educational and therapeutic programs that bring the world of nature into closed-care institutions.

The animals we bring are incorporated into these representations of environments, so that the animals' natural context becomes clearer.

As the themes build in layers upon one another, the metaphors inherent in these themes become the undergirding for the intermediary experience to occur. The heart of it all is building a shared context, one that links our human experience with the wider scope of the natural world. Brought indoors, the meadow or the marsh or the forest's edge can gently transform the institutional setting with a sense of the wild.

Animals As Intermediaries grew out of a belief that we are all connected through nature, that this connection can restore a sense of wholeness and a sense of place, and that this connection is both elemental and essential. Having knowledge of the natural cycles and seasons can give us the context we need to come through difficulty.

Bring Me the Ocean

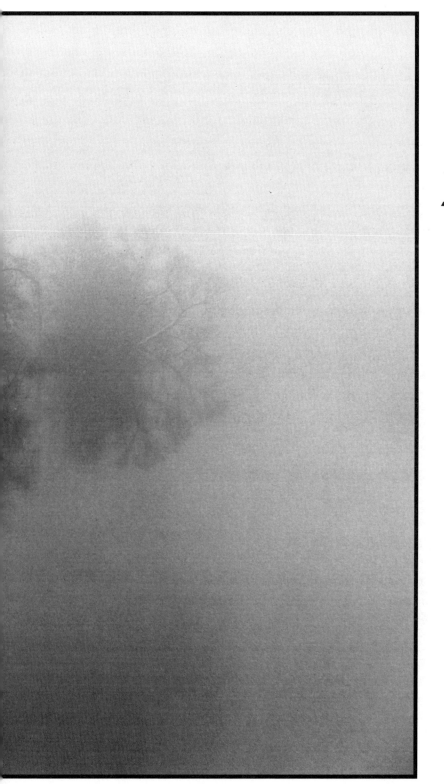

Fall

Fall Gatherings

We need the tonic of wildness,—to wade sometimes in marshes where the bittern and the meadow-hen lurk, and hear the booming of the snipe; to smell the whispering sedge where only some wilder and more solitary fowl builds her nest.... At the same time that we are earnest to explore and learn all things, we require that all things be mysterious and unexplorable, that land and sea be infinitely wild.... We can never have enough of nature.

—Henry David Thoreau, *Walden*

$\mathcal{M}$ORNING ARRIVES, A CRISP, chilly, fall morning. Sarah, Suzanne, and I eat an early breakfast, and the three of us set out down the back meadow to see what we can gather for our day's program.

This morning we will be bringing a fall meadow into a hospital school setting for elementary school children who have physical handicaps stemming from such difficulties as cerebral palsy, muscular dystrophy, and spina bifida. The majority of the children are in wheelchairs or bed carts, and many of them have difficulties with speech. With their age and handicaps in mind, we are gathering materials fresh from the meadow, and animals from our barn. We focus on sensory materials that will evoke the unspoken, on textures that do not need words. We will choose animals to bring that will carry metaphors correlating with the themes we have picked: fall, migration, burrowing, storing food, survival in winter. There is so much abundance in the fall that its sights and smells can renew, or create, a connection with the natural world. It is a season rich with metaphors for our lives.

As we walk, the mist is hanging thickly in the hollows of the meadow, and our boots catch in the mixture of mist and blackberry brambles. Near the edge of the red-maple swamp, I stumble in surprise, having stepped into a large moving shadow.

"Look up!" I call to the others, as I catch my breath under the broad wing strokes of a great blue heron. A pair of them has nested in the marsh for the last five years, but the sight of one flying overhead never fails to astound me.

We reach the edge of Secret Pond, a small polliwog haven tucked away behind the alder trees, and we find the cattails, tall and ruddy brown. The soft but compact "tail" of the cat will be a good contrast to the sharper edge of its stalk, so we gather several cattails from the thick cluster.

Nearby, milkweed pods are bursting open, their plumes ready to fly on the next gust of wind. Sarah adds some pods to the basket as she talks about seed distribution and we picture the children blowing milk-weeds. I pull from her curly hair several wayward fluffs. She begins forming a story for the children, tossing ideas out to us, like spider webs on the wind.

Just below the old willow tree we find a rare treasure—an oriole's broken nest. It lies on the ground, worn and tattered, after having swung at the end of its branch unused for two seasons. We've quietly yearned for it, watching where it swung, high over our heads in the willow, and wondering when a storm would bring it down.

We find a special treat of late blackberries, which don't quite make it as far as the basket. Continuing on, we find another gift, a red-tail hawk's feather, russet and fine. One of the animals we will be bringing to the hospital school is a southwestern bird, a permanently injured but otherwise healthy swainson's hawk. This morning's gathered red-tail feather will represent a northeastern hawk. Next we cut a bundle of dried grasses from the field as bedding for the rabbits we'll also be bringing.

At the edge of the meadow, where it meets the red-maple swamp, we find the cloven tracks of a large deer. Carefully digging up a circle of the claylike soil, we notice how the hooves have left a deep impression. By the size and depth of the tracks, we decide they have been made by a buck at full run.

"Are these from that handsome four-pronged buck we saw last week?" Suzanne asks. We reflexively look around, expecting to see the large buck materialize beside us out of the mist. We laugh as we catch ourselves doing this.

On we walk, the three of us selecting materials that will carry our theme of smelling and touching and hearing the meadow; finally, our baskets hold enough rich bounty. The mist begins to lift as the sun grows stronger.

The gathering time has been a chance for us to slow down and notice, to breathe the unique air of the meadow. We have gathered images as well. We will carry these fresh images with us into the institution, awake with our morning exploration and the surprises we have found. It is hard to turn back from such an outing.

At the house, we begin placing animals into their traveling cases. The rabbits go together, with their dried grasses. We slip the swainson's hawk sideways into her carrier, strong right wing first, protecting her permanently injured left wing, which was damaged in the wild many years ago and left her flightless. She settles herself in, shaking her wings out, and fluffing her feathers.

Two orphaned flying squirrels, who are with us until next spring, wriggle their wiry bodies around and flash large brown eyes. Into the van go our newly collected meadow materials as well as items from our stored supplies. We load up rocks of many sizes, a big hollow log, water, moss, vases to hold cattails, the skull of a deer, empty butterfly cocoons, dried seed pods that rattle loudly, and the lower jaw bone of a fox.

Lastly, our two dogs, Shadow and Fern, pile into the van, excited to be going to work. Tanga, our huge golden cat, unwinds himself from the couch, joining the burgeoning group.

At the hospital school we carry everything to the library. Laying tarps down on the floor, we begin literally to build the meadow from the ground up. The grasses weave a thick dry carpet, moss and rocks surround the logs, water swirls into a large platter with stones, and sturdy cattails stand up behind the log.

We place a wide two-foot-high circle of Plexiglas around the center of the meadow. Its clear shield will form a safe place for the rabbits to explore without risk of injury. It is also comforting to people who may not want animals to come near them. There is a clear boundary for both animal and individual. From this center, the meadow continues outward, stretching towards the gathering group, the materials enticing people to explore the meadow.

Branches of alder surround the outside of the Plexiglas, while baskets of fall harvest—pumpkins, squashes, corn, and gourds of all sizes—are woven into place with the bright joy of bittersweet vines around the borders of the tarp.

Before placing the rabbits in the center, we welcome everyone into a circle around the meadow. We greet people as they arrive, and give them the opportunity to say hello to the dogs if they choose to. We talk about how to create a "safe environment." This discussion allows participants their own degree of involvement. It gives them the opportunity to observe and to voice fears of animals. It builds an understanding of what safety means for both the animals and the participants.

Sarah opens with a story about harvest. We talk about the transition of fall into winter, the wind bringing the leaves down, the chill entering the air, and the animals preparing for the cold.

David, able only to move his head, strokes a rabbit with his cheek, gently smoothing back her fur. As Tanga lounges on top of Mike's communication board, Mike listens closely to the cat's heartbeat and, with one shaking finger, spells out "W-A-R-M!"

Emily prefers to stay far from the animals, cradling the round pumpkin instead, and sharing it with her friend Dan. Together they stroke the ridges of the pumpkin and laugh at the prickly fuzz of the stem.

We introduce the rabbits to their habitat, where they explore, nibble on grasses, drink water from the platter, and leap through and over the hollow log.

Before she brings in the swainson's hawk, Suzanne prepares a time of stillness in the room. She asks what the hawk might need to feel safe, what the children also need to feel safe. The children offer ideas of quiet and stillness, and one child says "love." As Suzanne invites the hawk onto her leather glove, Sarah creates a forest with the children, and they become quiet like pine trees on a windless day. The presence of the hawk further silences us.

The deep mud track of the buck that we dug up from the meadow leads to another story we imagine together, in which we hear the buck go rushing through the swamp grasses and see him leap the brook, traveling through the dusk. Everything from the simplest seed to the strength of the hawk leads into another aspect of autumn patterns.

Later, Sarah brings out a once-living green heron. A friend of ours carefully preserved this dead heron, which allows us to look more closely at the wing structures, even to touch gently the breastbone and feathers of a bird—something that is not possible with the live hawk. The heron's wings have been spread wide, so the iridescent greens shine in the light, multihued.

One young girl, lying in a bed cart with her arms strapped outspread on the sheets above her head, looks over at the heron, and indicating her own arched and widespread arms with a gesture of her chin, says with a smile, "I have a large wingspan too!"

A young tree is shown around, its roots held in burlap so that it can be seen top to bottom before being replanted. A young girl who is blind strokes the roots and says, *"Now* I see how a tree stands! I've never seen roots before."

All through autumn we hear a double voice: one says everything is ripe; the other says everything is dying.

—Gretel Ehrlich, *The Solace of Open Spaces*

The fall in particular offers a rich program, one that leads us into all the other seasons. It is a combination of the life-giving qualities of harvest and bounty, and the time of dying back and entering winter. It is the season that most reminds me of patterns and cycles, and of transition.

Inner City

𝒜RRIVING AT AN AIDS CHRONIC CARE FACILITY in an inner-city hospital for young children, we transfer our autumn materials to a trucking cart and wheel it into the hospital. Inside we shift everything again, this time onto a gurney. On this stainless steel cart, ordinarily used for bodies, we pile our bounty: pumpkins, hollow logs, grapevines, ducks, rabbits, gourds, cattails, milkweed pods, pine needles, and stones.

Wheeling this unusual, burgeoning gurney through the stark halls of the hospital, I have the urge to call out, "Emergency! Mother Nature coming through!" In the elevator, with ducks quacking and bunnies scuffling, a new voice enters the hospital with us—the very alive voice of nature.

Eight frail children come into the meeting room, their eyes widening as they follow the path of pine boughs. The pungent, crisp scent of crushed pine needles rises into the hospital air. The children gather into a small circle. Seated in the laps of staff members, they reach for our hands.

Together we walk through fall. It is the first time most of them have seen a sunflower, or an ear of corn unhusked and on its stalk. Sadly, it may be the only time for these very ill children.

We build a meadow together. Children who are able to, choose something to carry into the center of the grassy circle. As each piece is added—the hollow log, the stones, the water, the milkweed—the meadow grows. Gradually the meadow takes form, replete with smells and textures.

The children ask questions about everything. Even in their illness, they are thoroughly kids. Upon finding that milkweed seeds float on their breath, they blow clouds of them up into the air, laughing as fluff drifts back down and lands on their heads.

Shaking tall stalks of corn, we talk about the wind running through the dry cornfield. The youngest and sickest child, Jenny, lies listlessly in her nurse's lap, eyes half closed. But when we pass her two pods of honey locust, she grasps one in each of her hands, and suddenly raises her arms into the air to shake the dried pods with great energy and the most incredible smile of joy.

Small, fragile Elaine holds a huge yellow sunflower up next to her face, like two suns meeting. The memory warms us on our drive home.

These children were born HIV-positive, and several were abandoned shortly after the diagnosis. They are extremely sick and most of them will continue to live within institutional walls for their short lives. Even so, they are kids like any others. Their illness would seem to exclude the possibility of light and humor, and yet they shine through all labels, reaching for an animal or piece of nature with the particular intense curiosity of children.

12 Fall

Fear

*F*EAR: THE BOUNDARY, THE CATALYST. There are times when fear overcomes us, times when we overcome fear.

Our glorious gopher snake, five feet of sinuous, cool muscle, is a terrifying creature to many people. Stereotypically one of the most feared of our animals, she is also responsible for some of the most dramatic changes that we see.

One image in particular stands out: John, with his sweatshirt sleeve stretched down to cover his hand and with his hood pulled tightly over his face, slowly approaching the snake. His fear hung in the air, palpable. He had the choice to leave the room or stay at a distance, but somehow he was drawn toward the snake, as if magnetized to touch her, to touch his fear.

It was a desert program.

We talked about how the snake needed a safe place to be in the room with all these people, in unspoken parallel to the boys' own need to feel safe. Trust and safety were key issues for these boys, whose emotional and learning difficulties were often interwoven with a history of violence.

We had been coming here for several years, so trust was already established, and the ground rules of choice were well known. Each boy expressed his interest or fear and made his need clear to us before we brought the snake into the room.

John knew us well enough by now to believe that we would not bring the snake close to him unless he asked. So he watched.

As he watched, the other boys joined their hands in a line of support for the snake's long body. John gradually drew near, listening to Suzanne explain how the snake was unsure of new people, how she was timid and was tasting the air with her tongue, "smelling" their scents.

Intrigued, he drew even closer, as if unaware how near he really was. He stopped and watched the smooth body of the snake as she eased in her methodical way from hand to hand. Then quietly, in the midst of the other boys, John reached out a cloaked hand and touched the snake. He touched his fear, and smiled.

Around John other changes were also occurring. The internal struggles among students in the class were continual, and rifts were constantly forming depending on who got along with whom, and who had hit whom recently. Yet in order to hold the snake safely, the boys had to put aside classroom competitions and angers. They knew that abruptly dropping a section of the snake's body could seriously injure her, so they had to work together. Each child's supporting hands were equally important. The extraordinary unified gentleness of the boys was moving to observe. The calm in the room after the snake left was a tribute to the depth of their experience.

There are many fears about animals, particularly about snakes and mice. When carefully presented, these creatures can inspire people to move through their fear to curiosity and understanding, even if fear remains.

Explaining the animal's own fears and needs often generates a new understanding and compassion. When introducing the owl and the hawk, we explain how direct, frontal staring at them is aggressive and that a sideways glancing may allow them to feel safer. Usually this description meets with a ripple of understanding, and a subtle gentleness enters the framework of interaction. We all know what it is like to be looked at confrontationally, and it is important to understand that, for most animals, looking head-on is a predator's stance.

A great many of these transformational moments have to do with the spirit with which an animal is presented. If one presents the snake as beautiful and holds her as a special, alive creature, new understanding develops, and fear may gradually diminish. The consideration and gentleness required to create a safe environment apply to the participants as well as to the animals and materials. An animal or material is brought to a participant only with his or her consent. At any time he or she may choose to say no to seeing, touching, or even being in the same room. It is as important to have choice as it is to participate.

A catalyst that equals the strength of fear is laughter. Laughter can neutralize, unify, and uplift interaction. Animals offer a great chance to loosen up and laugh. Pigs are particularly helpful in this. One morning at this same institution, the boys joined together to help contain a pig in a circle. The pig was snouty and squiggly and splendid as only a pig can be. Young and affectionate, she nudged right up to the children. The tarps were all laid carefully in the middle of the circle—rug risk management. She quietly snorted her way around the group, snuffling with each new smell, until she changed her mind and bolted free, running from the circle. Pigs can be hard to stop, especially when they want to go somewhere. Reaching the other side of the room, she signed her victory dash with a heap of pig dung, all over one of the new rugs. The protective tarps stayed nice and unsoiled, safe in the circle of exuberantly laughing boys.

Choices

*T*HROUGH WORKING WITH ANIMALS and natural materials, an individual has many choices about how, or with whom, to relate. Interaction on a therapeutic and social level can be broadened by using the gentle bridges of the intermediary animal or material.

We were at a residential treatment center serving preadolescent boys with severe emotional disturbances and learning difficulties. Although I was new to the site, Animals As Intermediaries had been there on a monthly basis for several years.

As we began the hands-on part of the program, I found a place to sit on the floor with Fern, one of our dogs. Ten-year-old Nathan joined us there and began talking to Fern.

After petting her for a few moments, he began to talk to me about dogs and, soon, about death. He told me that he had once owned a dog, but that she had jumped off the porch while tied to her leash and had strangled to death.

He was the one who had tied her to the porch, and he was the one who had found her. Nathan described the experience vividly, talking in an open and vulnerable way about his intense guilt and grief.

We spoke for a long time. The program ended around us, and Nathan said good-bye to Fern.

After this program, during our staff discussion, John, the head teacher, said that in the three years Nathan had been with the school he had refused to speak with therapists, teachers, or classmates about his past or his family.

We hadn't known this, as we usually choose to work without learning case histories beforehand, unless there is a need to know. We prefer to meet the children or adults without bias. We are often surprised after a program to learn a history that we wouldn't have guessed from watching someone interact with an animal or a material.

The teacher asked about the dramatic change in Nathan's interaction, wondering what I had said to elicit such trust. I had said very little; it was Fern who had acted as the intermediary. Fern was the catalyst, and I was a listener.

There can be unspoken messages in interactions with people, judgment about the social structures and rules of what is acceptable and normal to say, express, or do. But animals don't demand such conformity of a person. Instead, they require only the respect, dignity, and safety that all of us want for ourselves. This is the crux of the intermediary process.

The dogs are the anchors of our programs. People expect them to be there, and look forward to their visits. As people grow to trust the dogs, they then gradually come to trust us, too, through our association with the dogs. The dogs are like references: in their trust and love of us, they are vouching for us to the people we are meeting.

The dogs are professionally trained to be working dogs. Chosen for their kind, gentle temperaments, they are trained specifically to work in institutions. This means they not only have good obedience skills, but they also have specialized skills, such as knowing how to approach a wheelchair. They have an extraordinary sensitivity and seem to know who really needs time with them. Often we've seen one of them seek out an individual, stopping by him or returning to him. We are no longer surprised to find out later that the individual has special needs or is attempting to overcome a very difficult history.

18 Fall

It's Real Life: A Teacher's Voice

"*I* HAVE ELEVEN KIDS IN MY CLASS," Joseph offered, "most of whom are residents here; they are residents because their homes are not safe."

Joseph's class was at the treatment center for boys with emotional disturbances and learning difficulties. We were beginning our first year there, working closely with the teachers. He and the other teachers worked with the boys to establish trust and overcome the violence and scarring most of these children had experienced. The classes were volatile. Tables and chairs were often thrown, and caretakers had to restrain boys physically. Chaos was the environment Joseph was working to calm.

With such constant violence, it was not possible initially to bring any animals. We worked for months just with natural materials until the groundwork of trust and the possibility of a safe environment were developed.

Gradually, we introduced the dogs. As our visits continued, the boys grew to know the dogs and to look forward to their visits. We were clear that it had to be safe enough in the classroom before any wildlife, such as the hawk, could be brought in. Joseph found the boys could practice self-restraint and nonviolence more successfully when presented with the hawk's own needs for safety rather than just with classroom rules of safety.

Far from the boys' range of experience, the hawk seemed to arouse an intense desire to learn stillness and patience. Joseph described their response: "These kids can't sit still and create a safe environment for grades; they can't do it for points; they can't do it for prizes. But they can do it when it's really needed, and it's needed for the animals. The hawk doesn't like abrupt movements, so they sit still. The hawk doesn't like a lot of noise, so they try to sit quietly. I've never seen them so calm!"

The boys had learned to create a safe environment in which to view the hawk—safe for her, safe for them.

Some of the boys even sat on their own hands because they were afraid they would be unable to hold still when the hawk came in the room. With their new awareness, they didn't want to scare her. Many of these boys had themselves been violent to animals, possibly in response to violence inflicted on them in their homes. Gradually, with the fine work of their teacher and the gentle bridging of the animals and materials, they were able to see their effect on another living creature. Joseph spoke of this evolution: "The goal during the program is to create a safe environment for the kids, for you, and for the creatures that you bring with you. That is a very empowering thing for the kids, to be able to create a safe environment. What you give the boys when you come in is the opportunity to give another creature what they really need for themselves."

With each program, a subtle shift began. Wildness recognized wildness, and in their new connection the boys found a kind of quietness and dignity and the beginning of newfound trust. "It's real life," Joseph explained, "it's right there for them; it's tangible—they can smell it and they can touch it, and they don't have to struggle for it, and they don't get tested on it. It's learning through experience, the living experience. We're giving them something they can hold onto, and that they can relive on their own at some point; it's there always."

By the end of the first year, the boys were able to go through a whole hour without disruption, a completely new experience for them. Joseph described this change: "It would have been chaotic, because morning is a very chaotic time and the kids would have been out of their seats and yelling and maybe arguing. But you would come in, and throughout the time that the program was going on, a sense of calm would come over the classroom. It was just such an amazing sense of calm."

After a year of programs, these same boys began serving as mentors for other classes, especially with the younger children. Students would assist us in presenting a program, and it soon became a sought-after privilege. Their teachers noted a marked change in the boys' attitudes before and after programs, particularly when out in the recess area.

Children who had previously stoned cats and birds began protecting birds' nests on the school grounds, and began educating other boys at the school who were not in our program. They rescued turtle eggs from being broken, roping off the area until the turtles hatched out. They set up observation sites to watch birds fledge from a nest they were protecting. Summarizing the development, Joseph explained: "That's the ultimate goal in teaching kids with emotional and learning problems—the experience where they feel like they're worthwhile and that they have the power to have a positive impact on the earth and the earth's creatures."

Dignity

Otis, the young screech owl, has a permanent wing injury that prevents him from living in the wild. During this morning's program he sits tall and noble on Nancy's hand, his diminutive height stretched to its utmost. He has been to this hospital school many times to visit the children.

Twelve-year-old Ben also sits up straighter than usual in his wheelchair, greeting his favorite visitor. Born with cerebral palsy, Ben has been even further injured by an accident in which his electric wheelchair tipped over.

Meeting the injured owl, Ben greets a kindred spirit in injury, recovery, and dignity, and shares his feelings with Otis.

"I'm sorry you were hurt. It's hard to be hurt. I know you are being taken care of." His quiet reflective words continue, "You are a beautiful, beautiful bird. You are beautiful, just the way you are."

Across the room Willie, the elderly chinchilla, was slowly roaming up Jay's lap into his arms. Jay was born with a combination of physical difficulties that limit his movements. His right hand is a metal hook; his left hand is a curved shape that cannot grasp. The chinchilla snuggled right up into the metal of Jay's prosthesis. "This is the first time in my life someone hasn't minded touching my hook," said Jay, looking up, his usually wry expression lit with a wide grin as the chinchilla tucked himself closer into Jay's arms.

We can find self-acceptance through the simple unconditional actions of an animal. In taking care of an animal, even if the care is just holding the animal for a few minutes, there are opportunities to feel responsible and giving. An animal doesn't mind if a person is missing a limb or does not speak. With an animal, we have the opportunity to feel whole, both physically and emotionally, freed for the moment from inner misgivings. We can learn about injury, fear, beauty, pride, integrity, wildness, affection, defense, respect—all of which correspond with aspects of ourselves. Through the human's automatic use of comparison and contrast, the animal is made an intermediary for learning about oneself and, ultimately, about acceptance.

Clouds!

James had been institutionalized since he was nine years old. When we met him, he was almost thirty-seven. He was born with limited use of only his upper extremities and so relied on a wheelchair.

For several years, he had refused speech therapy and was adamant about not participating in occupational therapy programs. He read constantly but spoke very little to others.

This was Animals As Intermediaries' first of a series of visits to this chronic care hospital, and we arrived with an October program, bringing the theme of changing seasons, clouds, and winter winds.

James sat, silent, giving us only the token presence of his body. He slumped down in his chair, staring at the floor. As the program began, Sarah talked about the kettling of hawks, their soaring and rising with wind currents, and about different types of clouds.

Looking up from his lap at one point, James saw the clouds Sarah was conjuring and became animated. In a tremulous bass voice, he called out, "Cumulus!"

At first as he told us about clouds, he was difficult to understand, but as we listened, he became even more animated, determined to communicate his knowledge of clouds. His knowledge, gained by extensive reading, had not been shared before. "Seeing" our clouds, however, sparked him to turn outward and share his inner knowledge. His inner clouds became a connection with the outer world.

From that day on, James began participating actively, asking staff at the hospital when we would next arrive. When we were there, he spoke to the animals and, through them, to us.

One day, a ring-necked dove climbed gently onto his shoulder. He grinned. "Look!" he called out, engaging everyone. "Look! There's a dove on my shoulder!"

Ten years later we received funding to go back for one visit to this same rehabilitation unit. I was amazed to see James with twenty other people waiting in the hall for the program to begin. I recognized him from the stories, and from some of our original video footage. I introduced myself to him, saying, "James, you know my mother. Ten years ago she came with doves to visit you." In my mind I was seeing the video of the dove walking up his shoulder and then after a moment flying up around his head. It was poignant to meet him.

James lifted his head. Nothing in his eyes indicated that he had understood me. He looked blankly at me, strapped into his wheelchair. Then with his left hand James traced a walking path up his arm to his shoulder, patted his right shoulder and clearly said, "Dove, dove on my shoulder." In a wide movement he threw his large hands into the air with a flutter, saying, "Dove flew."

Ten years later. We had the same pair of ring-necked doves with us on this fall program. He held one cupped gently in his hands. Quiet.

Winter

Winter Gatherings

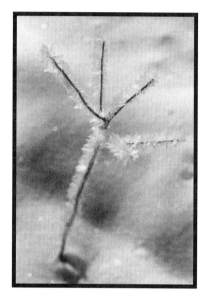

I like to remember during the daylight hours that the stars are still shining above me.

—Sarah Seabury Reynolds

*T*HE WINTER MEADOW APPEALS TO AN INNER PLACE. The trees are bare, the grasses are dried and bent over, their roots deep and resting, dormant. In winter we intuitively go to the roots of things, to the core of what holds us upright. The nature of winter in New England requires that we find this rooted quality, the endurance and acceptance that will carry us through these darker, colder times.

As we pass Secret Pond, we turn and walk farther into the red-maple swamp. We step from hummock to thick hummock, walking on the ice where it is strong and avoiding the open dark waters of Spencer Brook, which runs through the center of the marsh. The ice booms occasionally as it shifts, creating swamp thunder, and we hear the ice drop in a few places with a crashing sound, released from where it has been clinging around the base of a maple tree.

We break loose several slabs of marsh ice, with its stories of bugs and leaves and bits of swamp caught in frozen motion. It tells us about the edge of the meadow, where the marsh connects with upland. It tells us about freezing and thawing, for the layers of ice mark each flooding and recession of water.

We return home, not with the bounty of spring or fall, but with the sparse, bared-down quality of winter, which reveals a special kind of clarity.

We slide awkwardly across the driveway, our boots unable to grip on the black ice. Stretching up, trying not to slip, we reach to the eaves of the house to pluck icicles. Several cascade around my ears in that crystal crashing only icicles can make, and melting ice runs down my collar as I pack them up.

Our winter program will be at a chronic care facility for elders with emotional difficulties. With both age and injury, many of their senses have become limited.

From storage we choose natural materials that reflect the cycle of winter: the beaver sticks, stripped clean of their bark; the acorns half-eaten by squirrels and mice and chipmunks; deer's antlers that have been shed, their edges lacy with teeth marks made by mice. One can picture a hungry mouse searching for food under the snow and finding this treasure of minerals and calcium.

We also pack up our lively troop of domestic mice for the program, and a mouse skull, to compare the teeth with the marks on the antlers. We bring skulls and fossils of various other animals too. Bones and fossils offer us hints of history and the cycles of life.

Lastly we fill a tarpaulin with snow, to bring chills and joy into the institution. Winter has not really entered there, kept at bay by the artificial light and heat of an indoor facility. We bring many stories and songs on this program, an offering of hope; of coming through the cold, barren, wintry places of life; of coming through to spring.

Arriving, we spread a sheet of plastic on the floor. Here we lay down the winter world in its dormancy—the hollow log, the dry grasses, the pine cones, the tall, weedy stalks of fern. We spread a great wet layer of snow over this meadow, just as we had found the meadow covered outside.

As people gather around the circle, they place their canes and walkers next to themselves and greet our dogs Fern and Shadow with the joy of reunion. The dogs have been here many times over the last three years, and the reconnections are beautiful to watch.

Once everyone is settled, Sarah tells a Cherokee creation story: "In a time long ago, there was no light anywhere…. But Grandmother Spider was never lost, for she left a thread connecting herself with the past she knew, as she walked slowly through the darkness of a strange land she didn't know…. Finding the Sun, she brought a piece of it back with her, retracing her carefully laid thread, bringing the illumination into her life and the world."

After the story, we introduce other animals. The mice nudge Kevin's chin, and he laughs as their small, white whiskers tickle against his gray ones.

Sophie holds a dove on her finger. She smiles when it begins to preen its feathers, and she says, "Where I grew up, we raised doves and pigeons, my brother and I."

Hearing this, Matt smiles and nods, "My dog Red used to chase pigeons in the park. We walked there every day—morning, and again in the evening. I sure hope Red is okay. They wouldn't let me keep him when my son brought me here." His eyes wet, he hugs Fern, the collie, who snuggles in closer for more love.

We hold up ice, wet, as winter windows. We look at each other through the trapped bubbles. Anne-Marie laughs as the broad sheet of ice melts and cold water runs down her trembling arms. We speak of how winter turns water to ice, and here we turn ice back into water, a reminder of the spring thaw soon to come. The long icicles slim down in our warm grasp into tapered, light-catching clarity.

Sometimes we break ice, letting it slide into a crashing of crystal on the floor, to explore another kind of change, one we have heard out in the marsh when layers of ice crash down and melt.

For several people the ice becomes a mirror to memories, and they talk of skating and ice fishing on ponds and lakes. Michael speaks of skating on the rivers of Europe.

Janet leans out of her mobile bed to smell a pine bough, and comments on the fragrance of a winter's night, a sensory memory that rises up to her these many years later in the hospital. Ellen, for her part, protests that she cannot smell, so "don't bother to bring me the pine branch." But an instant later, she reaches out eagerly, gathering the branch to her face in the age-old gesture of savoring a smell—and says she *remembers* how good it smells.

We uncover the meadow hidden beneath the carpet of snow, lifting up the snow to explore the unseen, hidden under the seen.

As we gradually end the program, our friend Nancy Mattila brings out her concertina and sings a Gordon Bok song, with the chorus "The world is always turning towards the morning."

Back at home, we unpack and talk over the requests from participants and staff. It's already time to prepare for our next visit there.
They asked for lambs, polliwogs, and crows. They asked for spring!

A Wild Place

In the threshold between worlds, the fox appears and disappears. What seems a bundle of sunlit hay in a distant field uncurls, stretches, and becomes fire of red fox as she vanishes. Through our rehabilitation license for injured wildlife, a red fox became part of our lives for several years while she healed. As we sheltered her, she taught us about the wild place within ourselves.

—Sarah Seabury Reynolds

$\mathcal{F}$IREFLY LEAPT OUT OF HER BURROW, a brilliant flash of color on the new snow as she lightly trotted the length of her run.

Seeing her first red fox, six-year-old Amy asked, "Is she tame?" Firefly paused and in a lithe movement swung up onto her platform where she looked out from her run across the marsh. When she was an eight-week-old kit fox, her mother had been shot. Firefly was left orphaned. Injured, ill, and malnourished, she was found by a concerned farmer and placed in our care. The severity of her leg injuries meant that she would never again survive in the wild. Now two years old, she had grown into a lovely, brilliant fox and was the highlight of all our educational programs.

Amy stood quietly admiring the thick russet color of Firefly's winter coat, admiring her eyes, the black tips of her tawny ears, her movement and stillness. But not to be sidetracked by these other observations, Amy asked again, intently, "Is she tame?"

Sarah replied: "She knows us; we are familiar and trusted as we work with her and feed her, and the dogs play with her—yet even so, she still has, and will always have, a very wild place inside her. We need to respect this wildness."

Nodding, Amy thoughtfully watched Firefly for another moment. Then she amazed us all by turning to her mother and saying clearly in her young voice, "I have that place too, and you should know about it."

So often children are told to be tame, to walk instead of run, to be careful and quiet, to grow up, to be adult. Young as she was, Amy knew what it was to be tamed.

Hawk

*T*HE AMERICAN SOUTHWEST UNFURLED, in the middle of winter, in New England. A desert program. The children, aged six to ten, were from the surrounding community.

As we passed an aloe plant around, we broke off one piece and spread its thick, viscous juices on curious hands. A deer skull, cured hides of various western animals, sand, and dried flowers went hand-to-hand around the circle. We introduced people to baby mice and to our five-foot gopher snake. Stories that convey our connection with the natural world extended the discussion.

We were sitting on a rug in a circle of parents and children. One girl seemed separate, although her mother held her in her lap next to the other children. Jenny had been born with cerebral palsy, and its physical effects on her meant she moved to her own rhythm and seemed far away in a world of her own. We noticed that some of the other children seemed uncomfortable with her abrupt uncontrolled movements, unaccustomed to a peer like Jenny.

As the program continued, evoking the experiences of the desert environment, an attentive, respectful rapport developed, allowing the wildlife to be brought in. I brought the swainson's hawk quietly in on my gloved hand, her pride and dignity palpable in the room. Suzanne spoke about the hawk's permanent injury.

"Her fractured shoulder prevents her from flying well enough to hunt for her food and to migrate, yet even with this injury, she is whole, her spirit is whole."

Jenny's mother looked up at Suzanne, saying proudly, "Yes! That's how I see my daughter, that's my daughter—my daughter the hawk!"

After the program, as we packed up, Jenny and her mother stayed. Her mother talked about how the hawk's injury and dignity reinforced her own image of her daughter's dignity, giving her a new metaphor for her daughter's strength.

There can be great wholeness even in injury, and permanently injured wildlife offer powerful images of adapting to both injury and captivity while retaining inner spirit and dignity. But speaking about "wholeness" and "spirit" can be abstract. The wildlife give form to these notions. One learns from their presence, from their wordless clarity, from their wild integrity.

Simon

*W*E COME INDOORS BRINGING WINTER. Stamping the snow off our feet we enter the chronic care hospital, greeting the elders who have gathered for the morning program.

Some welcome us with great enthusiasm, while others are withdrawn and unresponsive. Simon is here. Silent Simon. He rarely speaks, tending to keep to himself. Today looks like no exception.

Blind and almost completely deaf, Simon is eighty years old. His hearing difficulties make it hard to converse with the other residents. Over the years he has developed a disinterested air toward hospital activities and people. He sits silently on the fringe of our circle, showing no interest in us, the animals, or the materials.

Mid-program, Suzanne comes around to each person, holding in her hands the thick leathers of an old draft horse harness. Reaching Simon, she gently shouts, "I've brought something from a friend's farm, Simon. Would you like to feel what it is?"

Simon noncommittally reaches out a listless hand and grasps a piece of the harness. A startling transformation takes place. Simon sits up, alert! His hands race along the length of leather, identifying it as absolutely as eyesight would.

With his whole body he reaches out to find the rest of the harness. Gathering all the heavy weight of the leather into his lap, he begins sorting it and laying it out as it would fall across the broad back of a horse.

"I'd know this anywhere!" he cries out. "I don't need my eyes to tell you what this is—I used to drive the ice wagons in New York City!"

Surprising everyone with his enthusiasm, he launches into sharing his vivid memories. Everyone stops to listen, for Simon has always kept his past private and unknown, yet now he pours it forth. For this afternoon, Simon has reached beyond his sight and hearing boundaries to relate to all of us.

After listening, other people share histories. As one memory continues to prompt another, a community of shared experience emerges.

Creating a community of experience is one of the simple effects of sharing the natural world. All too often in chronic care settings, an individual's focus becomes framed by pain or disappointments or the perpetual retelling of the same story. By bringing the natural world inside, an avenue is opened to other memories, and fresh stories emerge from the past or present. When we leave, and between our visits, staff and residents have the opportunity to talk about the commonality of their experiences during a program, or to share something they have rediscovered—the clouds, say, or the birds outside the window. New and old are honored in the present.

Simon 41

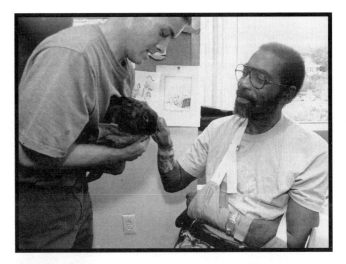

Stone Stories

*D*URING A PROGRAM FOR PARENTS AND CHILDREN, stones were passed around to tell "stone stories" with. One of the young boys had been told in school that he was a nonreader and a nonwriter. Initially he held back even from the stone in his hand, thinking if he couldn't read, how could he possibly tell a story?

As we sought to describe the ridges and edges of our stones, we shared an evolving story of each particular stone. Sarah said to the boy, "The stone already has the story, here, in the lines, the shape, the weight. Tell me about them." The child, forgetting that he was a non-reader, found page after page in his "book" that he could read to his mother, sitting next to him. Educational labels did not matter for the moment—he could read. This became a regular event for them; he found it was fun, finding things in nature to describe, and he gradually built on this new-found confidence to then read and write about nature.

In drawing such stories from the natural world, one can open an avenue for learning that can buffer and support standard approaches to learning.

Various forms of storytelling are a common thread in our programs. Storytelling can provide a safe way to rekindle fantasy, dreams, and imagination, to touch indirectly upon experiences of pain, growth, fear, loneliness, and joy. When told regularly, stories can become a reassuring ritual. At their richest, stories are drawn from many diverse cultural traditions, including those of our own families.

The stories become a weaving of animals and natural materials. Within a cultural context, they widen our understanding of the animals and materials. In telling a story from the Native American Navajo tradition involving a hawk, we convey an image of the way the hawk is viewed by the Navajo. In telling a story from the woven pattern of a cloth from Guatemala, we connect with both the culture and the material. The stories may be different or they may share themes, such as creation. Telling these stories from different cultures reveals diverse traditions and honors the varied ways humankind has interacted with the natural world. Everywhere we look, inside ourselves and around us, there are the traces of story imbedded in life.

When we present animal tracks, and fossils as "tracks through time," we focus on the story each plant and animal leaves through its impression on the earth. Living things create and leave some kind of story, perhaps by their footprints, perhaps by the disturbed condition of a place where they fought, rubbed their claws, died, gave birth, or fell into the mud. Even lichen will leave a subtle story on the rock as it very gradually wears the rock away.

One morning after listening to a story, Philip, a young boy in a residential hospital, sighed, shook his head, and said, "That sent shivers through me like an ocean wave."

Roots in the Ground

*F*OR JILLIE, THE RHYME "YOUR HEAD BONE's connected to your neck bone" had no meaning. The few words she used were unconnected, and she showed almost no capacity for linking meanings with words or for making phrases. She was thirteen years old, with severe cognitive and emotional challenges.

Searching for solutions, her family brought her to AAI, instead of AAI traveling to her. She first came in the spring. During an afternoon with our elderly dog Kelty, Jillie discovered that he would bring a stick repeatedly for her to throw. She was captivated by this, enjoying it so much that she played until Kelty was tired. Sarah showed Jillie how to ask the dog for "stick," and soon Jillie discovered that saying "stick" meant that Kelty would bring her the stick and the playing would begin. Day after day, Jillie and Kelty played. She had learned a new word and a simple linkage to an action. This soon led to a new chain of connection: as the physical act of throwing made her muscles sore, she began to correlate throwing the stick for the dog and the feeling of tiredness of her arms. Eventually, she even took note of the stick itself, and when it wore into pieces, she initiated the search for another so the game could go on. This very simple, repetitive act of playing stick with an old dog who loved the game was gradually teaching Jillie the link between actions, sensations, and words.

In the search for a stick, Jillie was finding another connection, that of the stick to its source. The search led her to find a tree with Sarah, and she held up her old stick, comparing the dead limb from the ground with the living branches that had leaves. She heard from Sarah that the tree grew in the ground with roots. They explored and found, in a bed of ferns by the tree, a thick root mounding and curving through the dark soil.

Summer came and went as she continued to play stick with Kelty. By fall she was taking more and more note of her surroundings, of the trees and other animals, with Kelty as her companion and guide.

By winter Jillie was putting occasional sentences together about things that had caught her interest. With Sarah she began carving wood printing blocks. She chose to carve the image of a tree, making broad roots into the snow around the base of her tree. As she slowly carved, she said her longest connected phrases: "Has its roots in the ground. Has its arms up to catch the snow."

54 Winter

Wings

$\mathcal{A}$NOTHER COLD WINTER DAY, SILENT OUTSIDE with a broad blanketing of snow. Indoors at the hospital school, it is loud with teenagers jostling between classes. As the wheelchairs gather in number, the jests multiply back and forth with the bravado of teenage humor.

A different bonding, one of awareness and intensity, becomes apparent when the animals come out and the questions begin. Silence greets the owl as everyone creates the needed quiet environment for her. As the barred owl turns her head 180 degrees, tracking the location of the newest voice, Jane asks about her missing left wing. "Can she grow her arm back? Will she ever fly?" The question is poignant. Jane's own thin arms lie unresponsive on her chair. Paul, another student, listens intently, his left arm replaced by a prosthesis.

"No, her wing will never grow back," Suzanne explains, "but she has become strong and has learned other ways to get around. She uses her tail, the way she is doing now, as a counterbalance for her missing wing, and she hops with a new sense of balance. We've designed a special system of perches so that she can become stronger and confident."

The owl sends her own silent message to the children, one of vitality despite injury. She has adapted to her injury and is completely *Owl*. The intensity of her gaze directly challenges the fact of her disability.

Ice Windows

*W*E BRING IN ICE, SHEETS OF THICK MARSH ICE, already dripping from the warmth of the car even though we have wrapped them in wool blankets for insulation. At a therapeutic day school for children with serious emotional and neurological disorders, we spread out the magic of winter.

The children gasp at the cold miracle of ice. Holding up windows of it, they look at one another through its textured surface. Several of the children look into each other's eyes and laugh, the ice offering a safe lens to look through, making the eye contact that is rare for some.

Across the room, Matthew is frozen in the lap of his therapist-teacher, covering his eyes and screaming. Our staff member Julie intuitively knows to give him something he can control. While his teacher, Janet, speaks soothingly to him, Julie offers him her documentary camera to look through. He stops screaming, uncurls, and lets go of his teacher's hand. Taking up the camera with intense fascination, he holds it up to his eyes and looks through this other window, a safe lens. He is able to stay in the room, calmed by his curiosity and the sense of control he has over his own visual experience.

For us, creating safety is always an exploration into individual definitions. For one child it might be discussing the situation; for another it might be the way the room is designed or who is sitting nearby; for many it is nonverbal. We explore together to find a match that will both alleviate fear and support exploration.

Emphasis on creating a safe environment for animals and materials assures participants that the same care for safety applies to them.

Bobby stood in the corner of the room, his body rigid with tension. Here in a locked psychiatric assessment unit for children aged three to fifteen, his interest in the animals seemed particularly striking. He asked to hold a rabbit after our program, wanting individual time with her after the other children had left. He took the rabbit into his arms, but as he did his body tightened up even more. He was trying so hard to be in control and to do it right that he was clenching the rabbit too tightly. The rabbit responded to his grasp by struggling. Suzanne intervened, talking quietly all the while about moving his arm under the rabbit to support her hind legs and make her feel more secure, to loosen his grip so that she would be comfortable. "Relax, here in your shoulders." His shoulders eased in immediate response. "Now, your arms too." His arms softened. "Try relaxing your whole body and see what happens." He did this so instantly and thoroughly that we were surprised.

It was as if he just was waiting for permission, or a reason. The rabbit calmed in his now supportive arms and snuggled into his chest. He stroked her softly with one hand, smiling. He looked at us with understanding, saying, "She's much happier if I am calm and relaxed than if I hold her tightly." As he turned to show the staff how to hold the rabbit, we were struck by how smoothly he moved, his body now supple and gentled with the act of holding the young rabbit.

Eye of a Storm

*J*AKE KNEW VIOLENCE INTIMATELY. His parents had tied him with ropes to restrain him. He had thrown himself bodily from moving cars. By the age of ten he had been placed in an institution. There Jake began beating up other boys. Outdoors in the recreation area he broke tree limbs, and crushed baby birds in their nests.

We were warned about Jake and the thirteen boys in his class. Jake was not unusual. We could expect trouble: objects were frequently thrown, disruptions occurred every fifteen minutes, and staff were present at all times in the class to restrain the boys when violence broke out. Most of these boys bragged about killing dogs and cats and frogs. Why would they be any different with our animals? So we began gradually—to build our own trust and theirs.

We worked closely with Diane, the teacher, to support her committed, daily work with the boys. Together we worked to set up a safe area, saying that we would only bring in an animal if the boys felt safe and if it was also safe for the animal. This led to curiosity, and together we built an understanding of what a safe environment was. First, some materials were brought in to be handled. Then the dogs began coming with us. Our dogs rapidly became a link of interest among Jake and other students, a rare time for them of noncompetitive interaction. With the help of the dogs' presence we laid the foundations of learning to touch gently, of learning to groom them with care for their joy and health. The students learned a new aspect of the language of body gesture, of subtle tones of voice.

Slowly the boys became more gentle, and the room would calm when we arrived. It was like entering the eye of a storm. We would hear the boys fighting and screaming as we walked down the hall, then for the animals they would quiet for an hour. For that window of time, the boys were calm and we worked together with the animals. It was an opportunity for the staff to observe their students, to see progress that they could continue to build on. Our visits were consistent, but, as visitors, we carried the unusual, eliciting a sort of behavior that could be applied to other class situations. This rapport gradually led to our being able to bring in the wildlife, and eventually, over the years, it led to the boys taking care of animals inside the institution.

After two years of working with the animals and natural materials, Jake described their effect on him to one of his teachers: "I think that it has changed me because now … I don't hurt animals anymore and play games with them and use them as target practice…. Now I try and help them. Now the animals come to me as if they know I'm not going to hurt them…. I can call a cat that doesn't even know me and it will come to me. I think they sense the way my attitude is. Like if I'm just doing that so they come to me and then I'll be mean to them, or if they know that it's a true feeling."

60 *Winter*

Bring Me the Ocean

"BRING ME THE OCEAN!" DECLARED JIM. Not the moon, not the stars—no, he wanted the ocean.

This was the second time Jim had asked for the ocean, and we were perplexed. How could we transport the ocean indoors to a chronic care hospital setting? When he asked again, Suzanne said, "How can we possibly bring you the ocean?"

"In buckets!" Jim replied, spelling it out letter by letter on his communication board. Several years before, while in his early thirties, Jim had suffered a head injury. The accident had left him triplegic and unable to communicate orally. He used a communication board on the armrests of his wheelchair to tell us his thoughts.

On our next visit we arrived with sloshing buckets full of salty Atlantic Ocean. Other pails held seaweed, mussels, clams, periwinkles, and a lobster—all on loan from the sea for the day.

Along with the hospital staff, we discovered what Jim had not yet told any of us. He had been a lobsterman prior to his injury. The ocean had been his livelihood. Every day in bad weather and good, he had been out on the ocean pulling up his line of lobster pots, sorting the catch and rebaiting the traps. A past emerged, and Jim showed us that anything, even the ocean, can be brought into an institution.

Over the years, requests such as Jim's have extended the scope of our programs, encouraging us to expand our own perception of what is possible. We started with the seasons of the meadow, then the forest, and soon we looked to the desert. Meeting Jim, we learned to bring the ocean.

Spring

Spring Gatherings

*The plants remind us of our roots in the earth and our aspira-
tions to the sun.*

—Sarah Seabury Reynolds

*I*T SEEMS AS IF OVERNIGHT THERE HAS BEEN a greening up. Shoots of new growth charge out of the soil, and crocuses burst into bloom beside the stone wall.

We gather up a bunch of pussy willow and forsythia, not yet open, and fresh shoots of grass. We find skunk cabbage, both plentiful and pungent!

The winter-beaten trails of rabbits stand out clearly in the meadow, intersecting the deeper trails of deer. Crossing both of these are the fairy tunnels, tunnels where the mice scooted through bent-over grasses and under blankets of snow.

We bring Owl; we bring ducklings, yellow and quacking; we bring baby-baby-baby bunnies in their nest box with their mother. It's a spring program at a therapeutic school for young children with emotional and neurological difficulties.

During the presentation of Owl, a young boy, Jeff, looks up as Owl sits on her log, blinking and gazing back at him. Jeff says, "Oh, thank you! I've never seen an owl in her woods before."

We've been coming here at three-month intervals, with the seasons. The sequencing of programs allows us to see the evolution of our work in combination with the extraordinary, dedicated work of the children's daily therapists and teachers.

At the first program last fall, Matthew had barely been able to stay in the room. Everything—even the inanimate materials—brought his fear to the surface. He left early in the first program. During the second program, in winter, he had the experience of watching the ice through the safety of Julie's camera and stayed longer. We have ducks with us on the third, spring program. When Matthew hears the ducklings quack, he begins to scream. But hearing his teacher-therapist, Mark, encouraging him to listen, he gradually quiets—and then smiles as Mark works closely with him in gentle rapport, assisting him in interpreting the experience.

By the end of this program he has taken a dramatic step forward. Suzanne brings the five-foot-long gopher snake out and holds her in her lap. The children come individually, or with a therapist or teacher, and see or touch the snake if they wish to.

Matthew does a remarkable thing. He asks Mark to come forward with him toward the snake. He takes Mark's hand firmly in his own and guides Mark to touch the snake.

"It is the first time Matthew has ever initiated, ever taken charge of a situation," Mark says to us later. "Usually, I take his hand and guide him. This time, it was as if he slid his hand invisibly down inside my arm, and safely touched the snake through me!"

Stone Walls

*W*E ARRIVED AT THE HOSPITAL WITH SPRING and began planting violets, Johnny-jump-ups, and geraniums indoors with the elderly residents.

Bill, eighty years old, quietly dug his hands into the soil, planting violets in pots. As he worked, he began talking about his life before the institution. His voice carried the same sureness as his hands. "I once had a farm. I built all the stone walls on my one hundred acres, built them all myself. I ran fifty head of dairy cows, milked them every day for forty years. I planted fields in corn, hayed the other fields, and groomed all of them of rocks for the stone walls. Every spring there would be more rocks to weed. They'd come up like trolls, popping up out of the thawing ground, pushed upward by the frost heaves of winter. It was hard work. I loved my cows."

For the next half hour he re-created his farm for us. "I had a huge garden," he said, "I grew a few violets too. I had chickens." As he talked, he planted, gently pushing the earth around each set of roots.

Behind him, Lori, a staff member who had known him for ten years at the hospital, wept quietly. She knew what medicines he needed, knew what he would and wouldn't do in the hospital, but she and the other staff had not known about his farm, about his stone walls, about his cows.

Moments like this allow staff to reexperience their patients, to see them interacting in a fresh way with new experiences, eliciting the power of their memories and creating the strength of new, shared thoughts and stories. Being institutionalized removes people from their familiar surroundings—from their city block and the hot smell of tarmac; from the sounds of their own kitchens; from the feel of the wind or the ground under bare feet; from growing potatoes and sunflowers. The loss of familiar surroundings can be difficult. For many people, the natural world can offer a bridge linking past experiences with their new situation, and not just through nostalgia. The natural world brings the vibrancy of the past into the present.

70 *Spring*

Lesley

ON THE LOCKED CHILD-PSYCHIATRIC UNIT it seemed as if Lesley had become invisible. Unless you looked closely at the place where the eleven-year-old sat, you might not even see her, so well had she practiced vanishing.

A long shield of hair covered her face, and her crossed arms held her body contained and closed away from other people. Her voice, too, had gone into hiding; she had elected to be mute. Mute, invisible, contained, pallid. I did not have to know her case history to imagine it had been hard.

The two younger boys next to Lesley were very verbal by contrast, volunteering questions and information about the environment of spring they saw in front of them. When I reached Lesley they informed me that she didn't speak. So Fern and I paused, as I repeated my question to her, not assuming that she would respond but inviting her to meet Fern if she would like to. A thin hand dropped down near the collie, the only sign that the child had heard me. Fern moved in to the gesture, placing her head under Lesley's hand, leaning gently against her legs.

As the program continued, we brought ducklings, rabbits, rocks, spring flowers, and doves around to each child, inviting the child to smell, touch, and listen. Each time a hand would reach out from Lesley's spot to touch, her body would begin to turn a little, and it seemed to me that I could see her more clearly. She was becoming tangible. A young girl in a chair in a room.

After the program, we invited the children to stay for a visit with the animals if they chose to. Lesley moved out of her chair and over to the waiting dogs. She knelt on the floor and drew them to her, into her arms, hugging them close, burying her face in their warmth.

The staff psychiatrist came back later to tell us how extraordinary it was to see Lesley with the dogs. The doctor smiled with ideas about how to continue this unfolding. She spoke further about how difficult it can be to assess a child who is in crisis. Given only two weeks of time with each child on the unit, it was a challenge to see healthy possibilities in the midst of the crisis, to stay optimistic in the face of so much difficulty. Now to see the children interacting, laughing, asking bright questions, holding an animal gently, or passing a flower with care— these moments gave the psychiatrist renewed hope.

The AAI program affords daily staff the rare opportunity to step back and see new possibilities. At a school for emotionally troubled boys, a daily caretaker remarked on how healing it was for her to see her students as whole and healthy. She commented on the surprise of watching a boy handle a bunny very gently and caringly, the same boy who yesterday had kicked this caretaker ruthlessly, who frequently had to be physically restrained by the classroom attendant for his own safety and the safety of others. Daily in close proximity to his violence, she was pleased to observe him capable of gentleness.

A visiting program does not replace the dedicated work of therapists or teachers, but it can offer them unique support.

Secret Pond

*W*E COME BACK TO SECRET POND to collect a bowl of spring pond water. There at the edge of the meadow, edge of the swamp, in the shallow waters of the pond, are clusters of glistening polliwog eggs. Many of these dot the sides of the pond, testimony to the croaking deep voices of bullfrogs all last summer.

We take several small bundles of the eggs, cushioned in a cradle of new pond weed and last year's leaves, along with an aquarium of pond water full of all its other assorted wiggling, hatching life.

We send some of the polliwogs to the pediatric AIDS unit with friends who will keep a supply of fresh pond water and release the frogs once they've grown. The three- and four-year-old children draw pictures and watch the budding legs.

Another group of boys at a treatment center for children with emotional and learning difficulties tends a small bunch of polliwogs, charting their growth daily as a class project, which brings them together in observation. They decide to send some of their polliwogs over to a hospital school for children with cognitive and physical challenges, and the polliwogs soon become ambassadors between the two schools. The children at the hospital school write to the boys at the treatment center about the size and strength of the polliwogs. The boys at the treatment center write back with their questions.

When the day arrives for the polliwogs' release back into pond life, the students at the hospital school race down the path with their teacher on an expedition to the pond, a cavalcade of hand-driven and electric wheelchairs. They look one last look at the young frogs, admire their strong, kicking legs, and then release them into the pond to swim their way to freedom in the weeds.

The children return to the hospital school and write to the boys at the treatment center.

Something as simple as polliwogs created a bridge of experience between the students of two different institutions. The polliwogs were also a gradual way to introduce the experience of caretaking into these two environments. In both situations, for very different reasons, the students needed to learn how to be caretakers of other living things. In working with the polliwogs, they were able to take care of them and to see directly the physical growth of the polliwogs into frogs, a rather miraculous thing to watch.

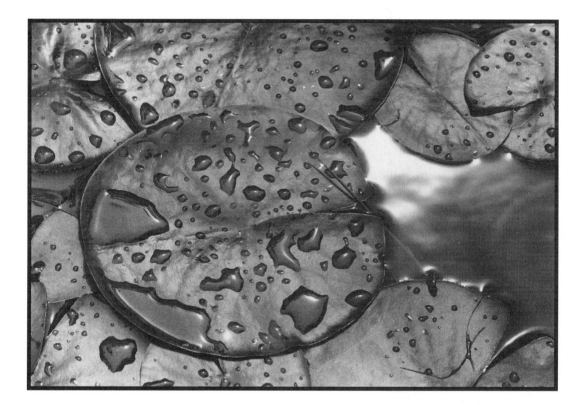

Farm

THE LAMB STOOD UNSTEADILY, LEANING A BIT against Earle's leg. Reaching down, Earle slipped a supportive arm under the lamb's belly while offering warm milk from a bottle. Earle is a friend of ours who runs a large working farm and has come with us on various programs.

As the lamb eagerly nursed, and rivulets of milk foamed up around his fuzzy mouth, Earle told the boys how he became the lamb's foster parent. He described how a ewe had rejected this lamb among her triplets because she was unable to care for them all. He explained about caring for sheep, giving the boys a feeling for cycles in the barnyard. "I'll foster this lamb until another ewe drops a stillborn or a sick lamb that doesn't survive. If she is lambless, I'll introduce this little fellow to the ewe, and she will usually accept him as her own and raise him. It all works out eventually, so I'm just a temporary caretaker till I can match him up with a new mom."

After the program finished, eleven-year-old Paul ran out of the room, extremely upset. He came back with the therapist and approached Earle. He asked, "Is it true what you said, about fostering and all, and what you said about rejection? Is that all true?" We learned that Paul had been placed in the institution by his mother after the birth of his twin sisters.

In answer to his question, Earle responded, "This happens most every spring when my lambs are born. I have a large flock, so it's bound to happen."

"Well, that's just like me," Paul said. "I was rejected when my sisters were born, and no one would adopt me." Then he turned to his therapist. "OK. I'm OK now. I've had two foster homes, but *now* I know I'll have an adoptive family of my own someday."

The conversation continued, with Paul, his teacher, and his therapist discussing how the school is similar to the farmer's role, caring for the children until they can find a good home.

The following year, Paul did indeed get his wish, and now has a home and a family. And as fate would have it, he was adopted by a farmer.

78 Spring

Unfolding

GENTLE CHANGES HAPPENED ONE MORNING in spring. Sitting together on the floor with their therapist, two girls became turtles of self-protection, wrapping their arms and legs into tight bundles, hiding their heads under the arms of the therapist. They were afraid of Fern and Shadow.

Keeping the two dogs on the far side of the room, Sarah assured them the dogs would come closer only if invited.

As other children interacted with the animals, Sarah asked Amy and Janet, "Would you like to see from a distance how the dogs tell each other what they need and how we can tell what they want?"

The girls hesitated for a moment, still tightly balled up, but their curiosity surfaced and they indicated to their therapist that they would like to see the dogs do this. "Seeing" became peeking out from under an arm, peering sideways at the dogs. Cautious. Ready to withdraw at any moment.

Keeping a ten-foot distance from the girls, Sarah began to work with Shadow, the young border collie. An intelligent and responsive dog, he is ideal for such moments. Sarah demonstrated with Shadow a dog's different expressions for wanting to be patted, for being afraid or courageous, for being alert, for listening, for being sleepy. All his signals were nonverbal, conveyed by movements of his tail and ears and by facial expressions. Sarah recounted Shadow's history as a lost dog.

In their curiosity, the two girls began gradually to uncurl from their therapist, peering out intently to watch.

Sarah called quietly to Fern, the farm collie, bringing her over beside Shadow, still keeping a distance from the children. Fern licked Shadow's ear, and he reciprocated, their mutual affection plain to see. This sign of care seemed to intrigue the two girls.

Sarah asked them, "Would you like to see how Shadow has begun to learn to work with us?" After a moment, the therapist indicated that they would like to see him working.

Again, with Shadow across the room from the girls, Sarah showed them some responses. Shadow sat; then he walked with her, coming to heel. Then Sarah brought her hand down through the air in a silent "lie down" command, and Shadow dropped to the rug in a relaxed but listening posture. The girls watched attentively.

"They would like to have you bring the dog closer, passing by them," the therapist relayed to Sarah.

Sarah walked the dogs by at close heel.

"They would like you to come back and go by again."

They passed by again.

Amazingly, Amy broke her silence, saying in her own voice, "Come again." Both girls were sitting bolt upright, watching the dogs with curiosity.

Now Janet spoke up too, "Bring them even closer."

After a few more passes by, Sarah had the dogs lie down on the other side of the room, explaining that dogs, too, need some time out.

The girls nodded and asked with quick voices when the dogs would be back again.

Developing trust and understanding, in order to move through fear and into communication, can be this ordinary: asking someone what they need to feel safe, and respecting the request. The effect can be dramatic as the individual moves from a place of safety to one of relative risk, speaking, touching, or seeing in a way that he or she might not have dared previously.

Many children with neurological and emotional difficulties have trouble distinguishing fantasy from reality. At this specialized school, therapists and teachers frequently ask a child, "Is this real or pretend?" and "Is this really happening?"—thus engaging the child to determine for himself or herself what is real. For most of these children, reality has been painful or difficult, while fantasy has been an alluring haven.

Natural materials and animals can become vehicles for safely experiencing a tangible reality, while at the same time supporting the benefits of fantasy. When a child holds a thick pungent branch of cedar, or bites down on a tangy apple, or strokes the coat of a dog, the response is fairly rapid and clear: "Yes! This is real. Yes! This is happening now!"

82 Spring

Emerald Green Moss

Since the day of her admission to the nursing psychiatric ward, fifteen years before, Esther had not spoken.

On this initial visit to the ward, Suzanne and Sarah brought a spring forest program. They, along with members of the site staff, went around the circle of people, offering pine boughs, moss, bunches of pine needles, and various animals to be observed, smelled, and touched.

Esther sat silent, as usual, withdrawn and inexpressive. She was unmoved by the great horned owl, and she didn't even glance at the mice or the two dogs. Then Sarah came around with her palms full of thick green moss.

Reaching Esther, Sarah smelled the moss herself, saying, "Esther, would you like to smell the moss? It's still wet with last night's rainfall." To everyone's surprise, Esther responded. Reaching out with both hands, she took the moss and buried her face in the pungent, moist clump.

Then looking up, she exclaimed in a strong voice, "Emerald green moss!" She stared for an intense moment into Sarah's eyes, before dropping back into her deep silence. Around Esther, her daily caretakers became silent too.

For fifteen years no one had found a way to break Esther's silence or had heard her speak or had seen her look directly at another person. It was a moment of awakening for all of us. This moment supported and renewed the staff's interest in Esther as a person, showing that there was indeed an avenue to reach her, even in her place of extreme isolation. Esther was not interested in the animals, but somehow the moss touched her senses.

This experience with Esther in our first year was a pivotal event. People often say, "Oh, it's so wonderful that you bring animals in!" Equally important is bringing in the environment, interweaving layerings of materials and animals and stories, for these materials are the foundation for all the rest of life. Trying to explain why we lug rocks and water miles away to an institution is often difficult, but whenever we have a particularly strenuous day of gathering all the diverse materials and planning how to work them together into a comprehensive whole, we think of Esther, and know that it is worth the effort.

Gentle Hands

MIKE WAS BORN IN PRISON. Now five years old, he had already lived in twelve foster homes. He was in a state school for children with emotional difficulties when we met him.

Working with Mike was a challenge. Initially, he made it very difficult for us to leave at the end of a program. He would fall into a tantrum, grab onto one of the dogs, clutch and choke it tightly, refuse to let go. Our conflict lay in needing to keep the animals safe while developing Mike's trust.

Many of the children in this class had abused animals and had themselves been abused. The experience of trust and safety needed to be developed, both for themselves and for the animals. One particular day, the children were very restless. Their hands kept shooting up in a loud confusion of questions, startling the animals. The children were impatient and rough when they reached out to touch.

Suzanne stopped and said, "Talk to your hands. Ask your hands to please be patient, to please be gentle. These animals need you to be very gentle and calm in order for them to trust you and feel safe."

This surprised the children—they began to think about the animals' needs for safety as well as their own.

Suzanne continued talking about safety and care, and waited until she saw the children respond. Gradually, they became conscious of their hands, and of a new way of being with animals. The simplicity of Suzanne's request, a request that structured the animals' need for safety, gave the children a challenge to rise to.

Exhibiting a new sense of care for the first time, Mike walked over and hugged and stroked our dog Fern, touching and then letting go of her with newly gentled hands. Then he quietly kissed her forehead good-bye. Later, as he was walking to the washroom, he said to his hands, "Hands, you are beautiful. I'm not going to wash off the feel of Fern."

On this day, he had learned how to hold and keep the sweet sensation of caring. He had experienced the comfort of saying good-bye without the alarming sense of loss.

Runaways

SHADOW SHARED A COMMON TENDENCY with Ted. They were both run-aways. Shadow had recently come to us with the difficulties a stray dog can have. With the help of students like Ted, we were in the process of teaching Shadow basic obedience. Ted was in a specialized school for young boys with behavioral problems; he also had a history of running away from home and school.

As Ted was walking Shadow around the school yard, the clasp on the leash opened. Shadow seized the opportunity and raced off into the woods, scenting a rabbit or pretending to. Ted ran after him, crossing out of the school grounds, an action totally forbidden no matter the reason. Caught up in the responsibility of walking Shadow, an honor in his classroom, Ted was now unexpectedly trying to bring back a run-away dog.

Finally Ted did catch up with Shadow and they both came back, with Shadow looking only slightly chagrined and Ted vacillating between victory, fear of reprimand, and a new sensation. He said that for the first time in his life he knew what it felt like to be run away from. He spoke about feeling fear, and responsibility, and the realization and understanding of how his own past runnings-away might have affected other people.

Ocean

WE COVER THE CENTER OF THE LIBRARY FLOOR with canvas tarps, and then carry in buckets from the car and spread down a thick layer of sand, sweeping in wave patterns with our hands. Some salt marsh hay stands up bushily from this base. Moon snail shells are rolled into place, and a long line of horseshoe crab shells walks across the edge.

The ocean is arriving at the integrated kindergarten hospital. The children here are both able-bodied and physically challenged.

Children come in, some walking and others in their wheelchairs or bed carts. Together they form a circle around our ocean. The two dogs begin going from child to child, greeting them individually around the circle. We welcome each person by name.

We begin with a Native American story about creation—about Turtle bringing up the first clumps of earth from the bottom of the ocean. The story line weaves our ocean theme into place.

As the words fade into silence, Nancy steps forward with a song, her voice filling the room with ships and whales and salt spray.

With the themes fully set, we begin taking around shells, seaweed, sand, and plants. The teachers and caretakers join in, moving around the circle, working with each child. Salt water is tasted. The seaweed is smelled and popped, its slippery saltiness explored. Sand, to dive fingers into, comes by in a bowlful. Shells are cupped to ears, to hear the ocean waves resound.

A young boy named Tom leans forward, stretching with great difficulty, to reach a moon snail shell that has caught his eye. Keeping his grip tight on the shell, he slowly works his way back up to a sitting position—his body braces making each movement a long, difficult process. Six months ago we had been here at the hospital with a different ocean program. On that visit, a staff member had held a shell to Tom's ear. Four years old, he had first heard the magical whispery sound of the inner waves resounding in the shell.

I watch as Tom slowly, and painfully, brings the shell up to his ear, curling his whole body around the sound. Holding the shell close, he hears the waves again, just as he remembered them, and a dreamy smile comes to his face as he follows the sound.

It is his own moment, so I continue on by, carrying our quacking mallard duck to another child.

When we depart, we leave behind shells to be touched and listened to in the library, and tendrils of brine and song in the air.

Summer

Summer Gatherings

I had lifted up a fistful of that ground. I held it while that wild flight of south-bound warblers hurtled over me into the oncoming dark. There went phosphorus, there went iron, there went carbon, there beat the calcium in those hurrying wings…. I dropped my fistful of earth. I heard it roll inanimate back into the gully at the base of the hill: iron, carbon, the chemicals of life.

—Loren Eiseley, *The Star Thrower*

SUMMER, AND THE HEAT BEGINS TO BUILD, rounding out the impulsive rush of spring. Our focus shifts. Summer, with its heat, is a hard time for the animals to travel, and it does them good to rest for a few months, to play and recharge for the fall—so we do fewer visits into institutions until the fall weather begins cooling the air.

Our summer gatherings are different too. We still go to Secret Pond and Spencer Brook, to the meadow and the marsh, but now we return materials to the places where we found them, and we collect a few new ones. We go to conferences in the summer and search out information on wildlife, or stories to teach with. We select our sites for the fall and plan workshops. We raise funds for programs, and we return to the desk work that has been pushed aside. Perhaps the best of this season is the chance to renew ourselves—our thoughts, our ideas, our inspiration. If one is bringing a sense of renewal and reconnection to share with others, it is crucial to find it first in oneself.

In working with materials from the natural world—mosses, rocks, earth—we are working with the very lifeblood that supports animals, plants, and us. The materials, seemingly so inanimate, hold the ingredients of life. When we hold in our hands our essential components—the water, calcium, and iron that help make up our bodies—we can begin to imagine how interconnected all of life is.

Silent interactions with materials or animals, such as holding a rock in one's palm or stroking a feather or a dog, build connections that range beyond the realm of words. When we touch a fossil, we touch the shape of an ancient plant or animal; we have physical contact with death and with the past. Conversely, when we hold a young rabbit, we are in contact with life, the present and the future.

The skull of a creature offers a view inside the animal. Through the eye sockets there is a place of mystery, of a life once lived. There is also the future, for nutrients in the bone will fall back into the cycle of life; the carbon, nitrogen, and phosphorus of past creatures may return in the wing bone of a hawk or the eyelash of a mouse.

These experiences give us a tangible understanding of interconnection, linking our mind more directly with our senses. Engaged in the moment, through the vitality of the animals and materials, we are, through that moment, engaged with the world.

There is an odd, almost inexplicable form of hope that can return deep inside of us when we listen to the natural and perpetual rhythms around us. The cycles represented by the natural world—winters, birth, sunrise, new growth, migrations—echo inside each of us. These are our rhythms too, for in spite of all our humanness we are still elemental. Our culture places a strong emphasis on light, on daylight, on the known and visible. We are also told what is normal for people emotionally. The tendency is to disregard, or label as abnormal, the darker times, the bleakness we all experience during our lives. What of those times when we experience the shifting of emotion? What of those persons who enter dark times? In experiencing the natural world, we remember that the world is always half in darkness; even when the moon is full, part of the earth awaits its rising. Darkness, so seemingly other and foreign to us daytime dwellers, is a full part of the living world, always covering half the earth.

For people in emotional or physical dark times of fear, anger, or depression, awareness of the continuing, steady cycles around us can offer an assurance of the normalcy of our experiences. Being aware reminds us that darkness is part of a cycle, that we can move through it to lighter times. Another day is coming. Morning after night. Always.

When we are indoors most of the time, this circadian rhythm can become disturbed. In institutional settings the light, temperature, sound, and activity are controlled, so an artificial rhythm is established—a rhythm created with fluorescent light and with temperatures that do not fluctuate. Missing is the cool of a fall morning that signals the beginning of the season's change, and missing is the growing warmth in the day as the sun warms the earth. In losing these natural signals, we become removed from our knowledge of place and from our rhythm within the larger context of the natural world. For this reason it is nourishing to bring indoors the sensory richness of the outdoors, to bring inside the breath of the wild to renew our pulse with the world.

Nature is more than pussy willows, cattails, and bunny rabbits—it is also hard rocks, death, the violence of the hunters and the hunted, and the harshness of the seasons. In understanding this seeming harshness, we find the miracle of new growth even more profound. Where an old leaf has died and dropped away, the scar becomes the site where the new leaf growth will burst forth. After a tree falls to the ground, its rotting will give nourishment to the young seedlings. Not only do the rhythms give us a pattern to live with, but the very cycles themselves have an order, a logic, which balances somehow the seemingly arbitrary parts of our human lives. When the structures that exist in human culture lose their initial intent and meaning, the larger order, pattern, and rhythm of the natural world endures.

One of the gifts of natural materials is the way they hold in their form the history of their living and their origin. Learning how a rock holds the story of how it became solid—sedimentary, igneous, metamorphic—we can wonder at the drifting of sediment in the ocean or at the fire of the earth. Carrying a rock in your hand can be like carrying the bottom of the ocean, the top of a mountain, or the heart of the earth.

Years ago Sarah asked a veteran who had lost the use of his legs in war about his connection with nature. In response, the elderly Nantucket Islander gathered up his crutches and took Sarah on a walk along the beach. As his dog ran beside the surf's breaking edge, the man turned to Sarah with a smile and said, "Now you see my legs." They continued on down along the ocean. In front of them wild birds flew up, black-backed gulls, herring gulls, sandpipers, and terns. As the birds flew up around them he turned again to Sarah and said, "Now you see my soul."

The Peace of Wild Things

When despair for the world grows in me

and I wake in the night at the least sound

in fear of what my life and my children's lives may be,

I go and lie down where the wood drake

rests in his beauty on the water, and the great heron feeds.

I come into the peace of wild things

who do not tax their lives with forethought

of grief. I come into the presence of still water.

And I feel above me the day-blind stars

waiting with their light. For a time

I rest in the grace of the world, and am free.

—Wendell Berry

Afterword

The beginnings of Animals As Intermediaries goes back to the early 1970s. At that time Sarah Reynolds and Nancy Mattila ran a preschool in Concord, Massachusetts, dedicated to using the natural world, art, stories, and music to support the diverse needs of students. Eventually this teaching evolved into running workshops for parents and children to explore the natural world together, creating stories, music, writing, and artwork from their shared experiences. In the 1980s Sarah began learning the care and handling of injured wildlife at an Audubon center under the instruction of Jane Caulfield. There she met Suzanne Ballard and Nancy Ashkar, and together they designed the Animals As Intermediaries program that could travel to institutional settings.

It is Sarah's belief in the whole person, beyond labels, that is at the core of the experiences that AAI tries to make possible. Her own experience with labels and educational impediments committed her to helping others find the bridges to healing and growth that the natural world had offered her. In her own words:

"By the age of twelve, I had attended fourteen different schools. I was still unable to read and write. Finally, I was sent to live in Maine for a winter with the Towle family—Ruth, a teacher in a one-room school, and Everett, a trapper and guide. I quickly managed to find my way out of the schoolroom and into a new schoolroom, the outdoors, shadowing Everett's every move.

"From him I learned a different language, about tracking animals, their scents, and their calls. I learned in a manner that had nothing to do with reading and writing correctly, but had everything to do with sensory learning, with which I had no difficulties. I began for the first time to do well in something. Even the isolation and shyness I had developed in school became useful in this context. As we waited in silence for the red fox to pass by, stillness was very important.

"The knowledge Everett passed on to me was a complex blending of all learning modes: sight, sound, smell, taste, touch. He held my thoughts with the same care as he would hold a cold bird picked up from the storm-thrown snows. He could and did, on occasion, call a wild deer out of the woods, holding it still at the edge of the trees with his voice, as he held me in wonder and awe with his teachings. Everett taught me that there were many ways to read. We read the clouds, the trail left by a fox, the wind direction, and the changing signs of seasons. He opened a world where I could learn, where I was accepted, able, and most importantly, whole.

"What would later come to be understood as dyslexia provided an opportunity for me to use and develop my senses, to explore and to treasure the world outside of school. Very early, I discovered the power of animals, plants, and the ocean. I came to trust the natural world as a place to know and to be known. All children need a place to be heard and understood. I learned that the tides come in, that the seed grows, that the dark itself provides a place for the stars, that a chipmunk will investigate a very still child. I found reassurance in the patterns that my senses discovered."

Sarah's own experience and her understanding of the power of nature are the cornerstone of Animals As Intermediaries. The natural world is a bridge for learning, a place where we can see and be seen, a place of dynamic living. Bringing this dynamic living quality of the natural world indoors can provide a sense of connection for individuals, and it can be done in many ways. Although these programs are greatly enhanced by the wildlife, they can be done in an equally profound way with one rock or a single leaf. It is as simple as taking in a maple leaf and holding autumn in your hand. A leaf can represent the whole tree and bring with it the sound and smell and light of the forest. What is essential is that the person presenting the leaf describe his or her connection with it, to say something like, "I found this maple leaf on the way to my car. It reminds me of the forest and last night's rainfall. Would you like to hold it?" This links the leaf with the wider experience of the place, the weather, the season, and the listener.

Talking about clouds or looking at a leaf may not appear as dramatic as meeting a hawk for the first time, but it can quite simply and powerfully remind us of the larger natural world and imbue us with a sense of place and wholeness.

At one site, where we had been going to a locked psychiatric ward for three years, funding was cut back so that we were unable to continue at the site. Without the resources or space to house animals themselves, the staff began taking morning walks together and then describing these walks to the residents on the ward. They brought the clouds and the morning mist inside with them. It became a great joy to everyone. Simplicity and care are the core of it all.

INDEX